THE LITTLE BOOK OF

HERB

TIPS

William Fortt

THE LITTLE BOOK OF

HERB

TIPS

William Fortt

How can a man die who has sage
in his garden?

Arab proverb

1. When you've got the choice, use **fresh herbs** in cooking rather than dried. They **give a longer and more vivid flavour** to the dish – and a much better colour.

"Fresh herbs give a longer and more vivid flavour."

2. **Keep dried herbs in dark glass containers** with tight fitting lids. Thi will help to preserve the precious aromas and protect from light and moisture in the air.

"Keep dried herbs in dark glass containers.

3. **The very best place to store your dried herbs is in the freezer,** where their flavour will last longer. Remember to take out the container in plenty of time, so that it can warm to room temperature. This stops moisture from the warm air of the kitchen from condensing on the leaves.

"The very best place to store your dried herbs is in the freezer."

4. **Fresh herbs from hot countries,** such as basil, **hate the cold.** Shock from the chill of a refrigerator may ruin them, so keep them at room temperature – preferably with their stems in water.

"Fresh herbs from hot countries hate the cold.

5. **Some herbs are more suited to drying than others.** Those from dry Mediterranean areas, such as thyme, rosemary, oregano and bay leaf, keep much of their flavour in the drying process. Moister herbs, such as basil, tarragon and parsley, lose most of theirs.

"Some herbs are more suited to drying than others.

6.

In general, **add small-leaved fresh herbs to the dish near the end of the cooking time.** Prolonged heat tends to destroy many of the natural vitamins they contain. Herbs with bigger leaves can be cooked for longer.

"Add small-leaved fresh herbs to the dish near the end of the cooking time."

7.

The most important part of a herb is its aroma. Smell is a vital element in what we recognise as the 'flavour' of a dish. A herb's aromas are contained in chemicals which easily evaporate into the air (which is why we can smell them). So store them well away from heat or pressure, which will speed up this evaporation.

"The most important part of a herb is its aroma.

8. **Freezing is an effective way of preserving fresh herbs** – as long as you don't mind what they look like. The freezing creates ice crystals which damage the vegetable tissue, often making the herbs squashy and dark when they are defrosted.

"Freezing is an effective way of preserving fresh herbs."

9. **Most fresh herbs can be stored for a day or two in the fridge.** Put them in plastic bags but leave the ends open. This will prevent mould spores growing on the damp leaves.

Most fresh herbs can be stored for a day or two in the fridge.

10.

If you've got a garden, grow your own perennial herbs, which will give a supply year after year with minimal attention. Mint grows anywhere (though confine it in a pot). Sage, thyme, marjoram and rosemary are also pretty tough, and can make attractive bushes.

"If you've got a garden, grow your own perennial herbs."

11.

It's easy to dry your own garden herbs. The best season to harvest them is early summer, when the flavour is strongest. And the best time of day for cutting is mid-morning, after the dew has gone but before the sun is too hot.

"It's easy to dry your own garden herbs."

12.

Tie small-leaved herbs, such as thyme and marjoram, **in loose bundles. Hang them up to dry in a shady, warmish place indoors** (not too warm, or the aroma will disappear with the water). Wrap each bundle in muslin to keep off dust and insects.

"Tie small-leaved herbs in loose bundles. Hang them up to dry in a shady, warmish place indoors."

13. **Herbs such as coriander, dill and fennel can be harvested for their seeds in late summer.** Cut off the ripe seed-heads with a good length of stalk and hang up to dry. Then shake out the seeds onto a clean dry surface. Spread them out and leave to dry for another couple of hours before storing in a container.

"Herbs such as coriander, dill and fennel can be harvested for their seeds in late summer."

14. **Herbs with large leaves,** such as sage and mint, **need very careful drying.** Separate the leaves and spread them on a wire rack covered in muslin. Place in a dark, dry room for 2 or 3 weeks, gently turning them once or twice.

"Herbs with large leaves need very careful drying.

15. **Once your herbs are well dried, they need to be crushed.** Spread them out on a flat dry surface and run a rolling pin over them. Pick out the stalks and any other unwanted bits before you store them.

"Once your herbs are well dried, they need to be crushed."

16.

Always remember to label each of your herb jars. A lot of dried herbs can look the same to an inexperienced eye, and some smell remarkably similar. Correct labelling now will avoid confusion in 6 months' time.

"**Always remember to label each** of your herb jars."

17.

Home-dried herbs should keep their flavour for up to a year. But commercially dried herbs from a shop will probably be a few months old by the time you buy them. **Replace your supply every 6 months – at least.**

"Replace your supply every 6 months – at least.

18.

Feeling fragile, low or hung over? **This simple herb soup from the south of France is known to locals as 'life-saving boiled water' and is a superb tonic.** Peel and crush a whole head of garlic, then boil for 15 minutes with 1 litre (2 pints) of water, a handful of sage leaves, a bay leaf and a little olive oil and salt. Serve with toasted bread.

"This simple herb soup from the south of France is known to locals as 'life-saving boiled water' and is a superb tonic."

19.

Chop fresh herbs by hand with a sharp knife or a mezzaluna. Try to do this carefully and neatly. Wild chopping with a blunt edge will simply crush the herb's fibres and cause blackening. Whizzing in a food processor is even worse. This will mix in too much oxygen, and spoil the vivid aroma of the leaves.

"Chop fresh herbs by hand with a sharp knife.

20.

A ready supply of fresh parsley is a joy for any cook. **It's an annual plant, so you can grow your own parsley in pots or beds, indoors or out.** Only buy seeds of flat-leaved parsley (forget the curly kind) and soak them in cold water overnight to speed up germination. Sow a new batch every month, and you'll never run out.

"It's an annual plant, so you can grow your own parsley in pots or beds, indoors or out."

21.

A few leaves of basil transform many a salad. It is not too difficult to grow, although a very fussy plant. Sow seeds well spaced out in a pot on a sunny windowsill. Basil hates being fiddled with, so do not transplant the seedlings. If the plants get infested with aphids, put the pots outside for a few hours.

"A few leaves of basil transform many a salad."

22. **Make your own basil pesto** – it will be much better than anything in a jar. Put about 100g (3½oz) of fresh basil leaves in a food processor with 120ml (4fl oz) of olive oil, 25g (1oz) of pine nuts, 3 peeled cloves of garlic and a good pinch of salt. Blend briefly, then add about 50g (2oz) of grated Parmesan cheese and whizz again.

"**Make your own basil pesto.**"

23. Chervil is a strangely neglected herb. Both its leaves and flavour are very elegant and delicate, giving off a subtle hint of aniseed. But beware – it loses pungency very quickly with cooking. **Chervil adds a heavenly touch to uncomplicated dishes such as scrambled eggs and omelettes.**

"Chervil adds a heavenly touch to uncomplicated dishes such as scrambled eggs and omelettes."

24.

Bay trees are not just ornaments in hotel lobbies. A small bush will survive the winter outside if protected from the fiercest frosts, and **will give you a year-round supply of fresh bay leaves – a delight for any cook.** The leaves have a hundred uses, from flavouring meat stocks to burning on a barbecue.

"Bay trees will give you a year-round supply of fresh bay leaves – a delight for any cook."

25. **Poor Man's Potatoes is a Spanish dish which makes simple use of the potency of bay.** Sauté a sliced onion slowly in oil, adding a chopped green pepper and then 3 or 4 bay leaves. Put in roughly chopped potatoes (and chunks of ham or chorizo if available), cover and cook for 20 minutes.

"Poor Man's Potatoes is a Spanish dish which makes simple use of the potency of bay."

26.

Fresh herbs in a stuffing can transform a humdrum roast turkey. Sauté 2 chopped onions in plenty of butter and oil, then put in a bowl and mix with 450g (1lb) of breadcrumbs and lashings of chopped parsley, thyme, winter savory, marjoram, sage and lemon balm. When it's cold, stuff your bird.

"Fresh herbs in a stuffing can transform a humdrum roast turkey."

27. **When buying garlic,** check the quality carefully. By late winter, you will find a lot of bulbs drying up or going mouldy. **Give the heads a good squeeze.** If you feel anything soft or hollow, or see any black patches, don't buy them. Good quality garlic should be hard and even in colour.

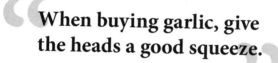

When buying garlic, give the heads a good squeeze.

28.

Peeling garlic can be a fiddly job.
Speed things up by first crushing the clove under the flat of the knife blade, pressing with the heel of your hand (carefully). You will hear a crunch as the garlic splits. Now slice off each end and the outer skin should come away easily.

"**Peeling garlic can be a fiddly job.**"

29. **Crush peeled garlic cloves with a pestle and mortar.** This will create the sweetest flavour. Avoid those two-handled garlic presses, which simply mangle the garlic and produce a much harsher result.

"Crush peeled garlic cloves with a pestle and mortar."

30.

A bouquet garni is one of the classic combinations of herbs in French cooking. Tie together a little bundle containing a bay leaf plus sprigs of thyme and parsley. This **can be used to flavour soups and stews** – and is easy to remove before serving.

"A bouquet garni can be used to flavour soups and stews."

31.

Fines herbes is a mixture of finely chopped chervil, parsley, tarragon and chives which **can be added to all kinds of delicate dishes.** Omelettes, grilled white fish and chicken can be transformed by its light touch.

"**Fines herbes can be added to all kinds of delicate dishes.**"

32. **Herbes de Provence** is a classic French combination. The mixture usually contains chopped rosemary, coriander, fennel, basil, thyme, marjoram and lavender (a surprising, potent and much neglected herb). They **are an essential flavouring for game or duck confit,** but try adding them to bread dough as well.

"Herbes de Provence are an essential flavouring for game or duck confit."

33.

The speediest of all pasta sauces calls for just 2 ingredients – fresh sage leaves and butter. Melt 110g (4oz) of unsalted butter over a gentle heat. When it froths, add a good handful or 2 of chopped sage and cook for 2 minutes. This sage butter is especially good for coating ravioli or tortellini.

"The speediest of all pasta sauces calls for just 2 ingredients – fresh sage leaves and butter."

34. **Spaghetti with fresh herbs is a simple classic.** While the pasta is boiling, fry sliced garlic in olive oil for 1 minute. Then bung in 2 handfuls of whatever herbs you fancy (choose 3 or 4 from parsley, marjoram, rosemary, oregano, rocket or basil). Cook for another minute. Drain the pasta (leaving enough water to moisten it) and stir into the sauce.

"Spaghetti with fresh herbs is a simple classic."

35. **Hyssop** is a sadly forgotten herb in most kitchens. But its unusual minty, mothbally smell and subtly bitter taste are worth discovering. It **adds a stunning new dimension to salads, and enhances the taste of rabbit stews and** (amazingly enough) **fruit pies.**

"Hyssop adds a stunning new dimension to salads, and enhances the taste of rabbit stews and fruit pies."

36. **Mint** in its many varieties **is easy to grow,** and has far more interesting uses than vinegary old mint sauce. It is an essential ingredient in the bulgur wheat salad tabbouleh, as well as chilled yoghurt and cucumber soup. Some vegetables go perfectly with mint, notably potatoes, fresh peas, courgettes and – best of all – aubergines.

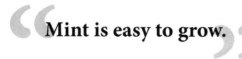

Mint is easy to grow.

37.

The people of Crete eat a lot of purslane – and their diet is said to be the healthiest in the world. **As well as having a deliciously citric taste, the fleshy leaves of purslane are a rich source of iron and omega-3** fatty acids. Eat them raw in salads, together with cucumber, parsley and tomatoes, with a yoghurt dressing.

"As well as having a deliciously citric taste, the fleshy leaves of purslane are a rich source of iron and omega-3.

38.

Basil wine is a traditional tonic from the south of France. **Soothing for the stomach, it also tastes amazingly good.** Pour a bottle of light red wine into a litre jar, and add a handful of basil leaves and a chunk of orange peel. Make 150ml (5fl oz) of sugar and water syrup and pour that in. Cork the bottle and leave for at least 3 weeks.

"Basil wine is soothing for the stomach, it also tastes amazingly good."

39.

Herbal teas are highly valued all over the world for their soothing and medicinal properties. Simply put your chosen herb (rosemary, lime flowers, camomile, sage or lavender seeds are among the best) into a warmed teapot. Pour on hot water and leave to infuse.

"Herbal teas are highly valued all over the world for their soothing and medicinal properties."

40.

Rosemary goes remarkably well with partridge. Put a good sprig inside each bird, then wrap them in bacon and brown in oil, surrounded with onions and more rosemary. Chuck in a glass of red wine and simmer for 15 minutes. Serve the birds with the strained and reduced sauce.

"Rosemary goes remarkably well with partridge.

41.

The volatile oils of herbs can be gently extracted by steeping them in vinegar. Tarragon, dill, thyme and rosemary are among the best for flavouring vinegar. Gently crush a handful of the herbs first, then place them in a jar (easier to fill than a bottle). Fill up with a good white wine vinegar, stopper tightly and leave for 1 month.

"The volatile oils of herbs can be gently extracted by steeping them in vinegar."

42.

Home-made horseradish sauce tastes far better than the commercial stuff. Peel and grate the horseradish root, then whizz in the food processor with lemon juice and cream. A little sugar broadens the flavour.

"Home-made horseradish
sauce tastes far better than the
commercial stuff."

43.

Dill is the quintessential herb for fish – most famously for gravlax, the Swedish version of pickled raw salmon. Mix 4 tablespoons of chopped dill with 2 tablespoons each of sea salt and sugar, plus a generous grinding of black pepper. Line a dish with clingfilm, lay salmon fillets on it, pour over the mixture and wrap the clingfilm round the fish. Refrigerate for at least 12 hours.

Dill is the quintessential herb for fish.

44.

The perfect tomato salsa can only be made with fresh coriander leaves.
Assemble your own from chopped onion, ripe tomatoes (skinned, deseeded and chopped), chopped mint, a couple of chopped green chillies, fresh lime juice, a pinch of sugar and a whole bunch of coriander. Blend in the processor if you like, but some like it coarse.

"The perfect tomato salsa can only be made with fresh coriander leaves.

45. **Always eat chives in their raw state**
– never cooked, because they lose
all their potency. Snip them up with
scissors onto salads or soups. Even
better, mix with sour cream or Greek
yoghurt to adorn baked potatoes.

"**Always eat chives in their raw state.**"

46. Keep an **aloe vera** plant in a pot on your kitchen windowsill. You can't actually eat it, but it **is wonderful for simple first aid.** If you scald or burn yourself, cut off the tip of a fleshy leaf and rub the cut end on the wound. You'll find it wonderfully soothing.

"Aloe vera is wonderful for simple first aid.

47. **If you are marinating fish** before grilling, **suit the herb to the variety** when you make the marinade. Fish with white flesh and delicate flavour, such as bass and bream, go best with feathery fennel leaves. Stronger-tasting fish, such as sardines or mackerel, need a punchier herb like oregano.

"If you are marinating fish, suit the herb to the variety.

48.

The best part of a borage plant is its splendid blue flowers. The **borage flowers add a hint of cucumbery glamour to salads and soups.** You can also freeze them inside ice cubes ready to pop into a jug of Pimms.

"Borage flowers add a hint of cucumbery glamour to salads and soups."

49.

Sorrel is a wonderfully bracing herb, with the tart flavour of spinach but more delicacy. It **goes perfectly with eggs.** Finely shred 300g (11oz) of young sorrel leaves and cook gently in butter until you have a smooth sauce. Stir in some double cream, season and pour over 6 hard-boiled eggs. Bake for about 15 minutes.

"**Sorrel goes perfectly with eggs.**"

50.

Watercress makes one of the best of all soups. Peel and chop 150g (5oz) of potatoes and an onion and boil in 600ml (1 pint) of water or chicken stock and an equal amount of cream milk. When the vegetables are soft, add 225g (8oz) of chopped watercress leaves. Cook for 5 more minutes, purée and season.

"Watercress makes one of the best of all soups.

William Fortt

William Fortt is **a gardener of long standing,** whose cottage garden in Wiltshire is famed for the beauty of its rare plants and the wonders of its many varieties of culinary and medicinal herbs. He has been an author for more than 30 years, with many books to his name.

"**A gardener of long standing.**"

Little Books of Tips from
Absolute Press

Aga
Allotment
Avocado
Beer
Cake Decorating
Cheese
Coffee
Fishing

Gardening
Gin
Golf
Herbs
Spice
Tea
Whisky
Wine

If you enjoyed this book, try...

THE LITTLE BOOK OF

GARDENING

TIPS

> Save your ice lolly sticks during the hot summer months. Next spring they will make perfectly-sized marker pegs.

> Empty plastic bottles make fine barriers against the curse of the slug.

Absolute Press
An imprint of Bloomsbury Publishing Plc

50 Bedford Square	1385 Broadway
London	New York
WC1B 3DP	NY 10018
UK	USA

www.bloomsbury.com
ABSOLUTE PRESS and the A. logo are trademarks of Bloomsbury Publishing Plc

First published in 2006
This edition printed 2017

A catalogue record for this book is available from the British Library.
Library of Congress Cataloguing-in-Publication data has been applied for.
ISBN 13: 9781472954633

Printed and bound in Spain by Tallers Grafics Soler